COOL ANIMA
IN THE AI
ON LAND A
IN THE SE

Speedy Publishing LLC
40 E. Main St. #1156
Newark, DE 19711
www.speedypublishing.com

Copyright 2015

All Rights reserved. No part of this book may be reproduced or used in any way or form or by any means whether electronic or mechanical, this means that you cannot record or photocopy any material ideas or tips that are provided in this book

Earth is home to about 1 million known animal species.

Lyrebirds are very common in forests throughout south eastern Australia. Lyrebirds are most notable for their superb ability to mimic natural and artificial sounds from their environment.

The peregrine falcon is renowned for its speed, reaching over 322 km/h while on a high speed dive. The the highest measured speed of a peregrine falcon is 389 km/h.

The rhinoceros beetles are among the largest of beetles. The rhino beetle is the strongest animal in the world. It can lift up to 850 times its own weight.

Basilisk lizard are endemic to southern Mexico, Central America, and northern South America. They are also known as the Jesus Christ Lizard because of their ability to walk on water.

The cheetah is the world's fastest land animal. They can reach a top speed of around 113 km per hour. The cheetah can reach its top speed in just 3 seconds.

Dolphins are believed to be very intelligent. When it's time to rest, dolphins will shut down only one hemisphere of its brain, and close the opposite eye.

The mimic octopus is capable of impersonating other local species or predators. They are notable for being able to change their skin color and texture in order to blend in with their environment.

Printed in Great Britain
by Amazon